D1268755

DISCARD

ASTRONAUT TRAVEL GUIDES

MERCURY AND VENUS

ISABEL THOMAS

Heinemann
LIBRARY
Chicago, Illinois

www.capstonepub.com
Visit our website to find out
more information about
Heinemann-Raintree books.

To order:
☎ Phone 800-747-4992
▭ Visit www.capstonepub.com
to browse our catalog and order online.

Edited by Nancy Dickmann and Laura Knowles
Designed by Steve Mead
Original illustrations © Capstone Global
    Library Ltd 2013
Picture research by Mica Brancic

Originated by Capstone Global Library Ltd
Printed and bound in China by CTPS

16 15 14 13 12
10 9 8 7 6 5 4 3 2 1

**Library of Congress Cataloging-in-
    Publication Data**
Thomas, Isabel, 1980-
   Mercury and Venus / Isabel Thomas.—1st ed.
       p. cm.—(Astronaut travel guides)
   Includes bibliographical references and index.
   ISBN 978-1-4109-4571-6 (hb)—ISBN 978-1-
4109-4580-8 (pb) 1. Mercury (Planet)—Juvenile
literature. 2. Venus (Planet)—Juvenile literature.
I. Title.
   QB611.T46 2013
   523.41—dc23   2011039057

Acknowledgements
We would like to thank the following for
permission to reproduce photographs: Alamy
p. 6 (© The Print Collector); Brown University
p. 17 (Vernadsky Institute/O. de Goursac);
Corbis pp. 8 (The Art Archive/© Alfredo Dagli
Orti), 23 (Sygma/© Tony Korody), 38 (© kyodo/
Xinhua Press); ESA pp. 5 bottom and 34, 39
(Astrium); Getty Images p. 29 (De Agostini/DEA
/D'ARCO EDITORI); © Jia Hao p. 7; NASA pp.
4 (© Calvin J Hamilton), 5 top and 16 (Johns
Hopkins University Applied Physics Laboratory),
10 (Ames Research Center), 12, 14 (JPL), 18,
25 (JPL-Caltech/University of Arizona), 28 (Johns
Hopkins University Applied Physics Laboratory/
Arizona State University/Carnegie Institution
of Washington. Image reproduced courtesy of
Science/AAAS.), 30 (JPL), 31, 32, 33 (JPL), 37
(JPL/USGS); Science Photo Library pp. 9 (David
Parker), 19 (Christian Darkin), 21 (Detlev Van
Ravenswaay), 26 (Walter Myers); Shutterstock
pp. 40-41 (© Martiin || Fluidworkshop); The
Bridgeman Art Library p. 11 (National Geographic
Society/Jean-Leon Huens).

Design image elements reproduced with
permission of Shutterstock/© Benjamin Haas/
© Luis Stortini Sabor aka Cvadrat/© Mopic/
© Stephen Coburn.

Cover photograph of a 3D perspective View
of the Eistla Region of Venus reproduced with
permission of NASA.

We would like to thank Mark Thompson, Paolo
Nespoli, and ESA for their invaluable help in the
preparation of this book.

Every effort has been made to contact copyright
holders of material reproduced in this book.
Any omissions will be rectified in subsequent
printings if notice is given to the publisher.

CONTENTS

Some words are shown in bold, **like this**. You can find out what they mean by looking in the glossary.

DON'T FORGET

These boxes will remind you what you need to take with you on your big adventure.

NUMBER CRUNCHING

Don't miss these little chunks of data as you speed through the travel guide!

AMAZING FACTS

You need to know these fascinating facts to get the most out of your space safari!

WHO'S WHO?

Find out about the space explorers who have studied the universe in the past and today.

VISITING MERCURY AND VENUS

Adventurous astronauts will love visiting Mercury and Venus. From chilly **craters** to violent volcanoes, these planets are packed with spectacular sights.

Be prepared for incredible heat and for clouds made of acid on Venus.

WHERE ARE THEY?

Mercury and Venus are the only planets in our **solar system** that are closer to the Sun than Earth is. This makes them seriously hot! Mercury is the closest planet to the Sun, and it is only slightly larger than our Moon. Venus is Earth's closest neighbor and is around the same size as our planet. Most of the unmanned spacecraft that visit Mercury and Venus take in both planets in a single trip.

WHY GO?

Along with Earth and Mars, Mercury and Venus are known as the rocky planets. Like Earth, they both have a solid, rocky surface that an astronaut can walk on. But when you step out of your spaceship, you will discover two very different worlds.

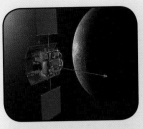

See pages 14–17 to find out which spacecraft have visited Mercury and Venus.

Discover what the **atmosphere** is like on Venus on pages 26–27.

Meet astronaut Paolo Nespoli on page 34.

NUMBER CRUNCHING

Compared to most planets, Venus is a short hop away from Earth. In 2005, the space **probe** *Venus Express* made the journey to Venus in 155 days. It will take you longer to get to Mercury. The *Mercury Messenger* probe, launched in August 2004, reached the planet in January 2008.

EXPLORING MERCURY AND VENUS FROM EARTH

It is not just astronauts who are interested in Mercury and Venus. Humans have been gazing at the planets and trying to uncover their secrets for thousands of years.

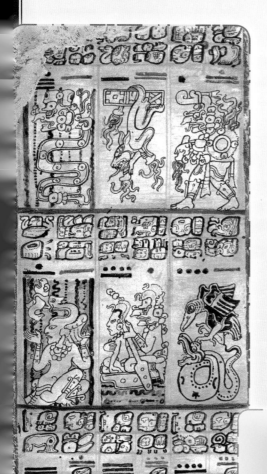

EARLY ASTROLOGY

Mercury and Venus can be spotted from Earth in the evening and early morning. They look like very large, bright stars. Ancient peoples did not know what planets and stars were, but they began to notice patterns in their movements across the sky. They recorded the patterns and used the **data** to create calendars and to try to predict the future. This is known as astrology.

More than 2,500 years ago, the Mayans believed that Venus was as important as the Sun. They called the planet *Xux Ek*, meaning the "Great Star," and kept careful records of when it appeared in the sky.

NAMING THE PLANETS

Many ancient cultures linked the objects they saw in the sky to religion. Early **astronomers** were often priests, and the planets were named after gods and goddesses.

The names that we use today come from Roman **mythology**. Mercury was the Roman messenger god who wore winged sandals so he could speed through the sky. This name suits the planet Mercury because it also moves quickly across the sky. Sunlight bounces off thick clouds around Venus, making it look like a beautiful shining star. It is named after the Roman goddess of love and beauty.

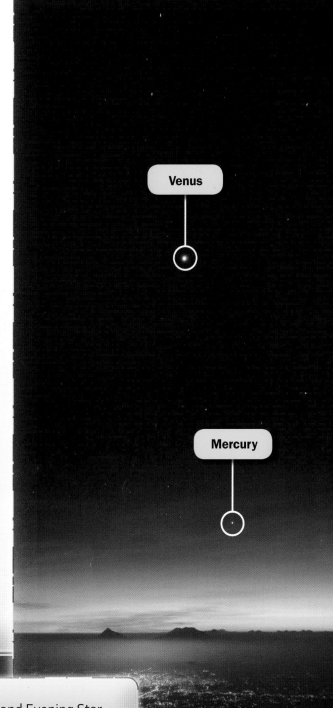

Venus

Mercury

Venus was known as the Morning Star and Evening Star because it looks so bright in the sky at dawn and dusk. Mercury is much harder to spot.

THE SCIENCE OF ASTRONOMY

Although the movement of planets cannot be used to predict human events, the information collected by early astrologers was very useful. Astronomers used it to discover new things about the planets and Earth itself.

GREEK STAR-GAZING

From around 450 BCE, the ancient Greeks changed how the planets and stars were studied. Many Greek astronomers were mathematicians. They came up with new ideas about what Mercury and Venus were and why they appeared to move through the sky. Some of their ideas were right, but others we now know were wrong.

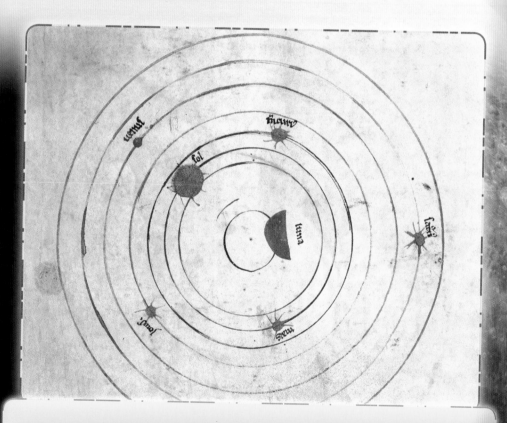

Greek astronomer Ptolemy wrongly thought that the planets, Sun, Moon, and stars traveled around Earth. This idea lasted for 1,400 years!

ARABIC SCHOLARS

From the 600s CE, Arabic astronomers made many important discoveries. They studied ancient Greek ideas about the solar system. They built huge **observatories**. The most famous Arab astronomer is al-Battani. He made superb **instruments** to track the movement of planets and figure out their positions.

COPERNICUS AND KEPLER

Al-Battani's work was very helpful to European scientists. In the 1500s, Nicolaus Copernicus made a huge breakthrough. He suggested that the planets, including Earth, actually traveled around the Sun.

Later, the scientist Johannes Kepler combined Copernicus's ideas with accurate data to explain how the planets move through space. This can be used to predict where Mercury and Venus will be at any time— which is important information for a modern-day astronaut trying to get there!

Astrolabes were the laptop computers of the past! They were used to measure the position of objects in the sky and tell the time of the day or year.

WHO'S WHO?

The Greek mathematician Pythagoras (c. 580–c.500 BCE) noticed that the Morning Star and Evening Star were actually the same object: Venus. He was also probably the first to suggest that all planets are spheres (ball-shaped).

A BETTER VIEW OF THE PLANETS

Until the 1600s, astronomers could only see the planets as well as you can see them with your eyes. When the **telescope** was invented in 1609, it was suddenly possible to make planets and stars look much nearer. This allowed scientists to see surprising new details.

In 1610, Galileo Galilei used telescopes to make an amazing discovery. He saw that Venus had phases (meaning it appeared to change shape) like the Moon. Galileo knew that this could only happen if planets **orbit** the Sun, not Earth. He had proved that Copernicus was right.

Through his telescopes, Galileo could see different amounts of Venus's sunlit side at different times. The race was now on to invent better telescopes and make new findings.

NEW DISCOVERIES

During the 1800s, astronomers developed instruments and techniques that helped them to discover more about planets. From the 1850s, people used cameras to record the images seen through telescopes, instead of drawing them by hand. Enough detail could be seen to create rough maps of Mercury's surface. But even though Venus is closer to Earth than Mercury, the surface of Venus remained a mystery, hidden behind its thick clouds.

Astronomers began to explore the **universe** beyond our solar system. However, an exciting development would soon bring attention back to Mercury, Venus, and the other planets: space travel.

WHO'S WHO?

Italian scientist Galileo Galilei (1564–1642) was the first person to use telescopes to study the sky. His proof that planets orbit the Sun went against the beliefs of the Roman Catholic Church, which was very powerful at that time. In 1633, Galileo was put on trial and ordered to stay inside his house for the rest of his life.

INTERVIEW WITH AN ASTRONOMER

Mark Thompson has been an amateur astronomer for 20 years. He has also hosted television shows about stars and space, helping adults and young people to understand the night sky.

Q *What made you want to be an astronomer in the first place?*

A I think it was actually a view of Saturn through a telescope. My dad took me to my local observatory when I was probably about 10 years old. As luck would have it, I got to see Saturn through a telescope, and to see it for real— it wasn't in a book, it wasn't on a TV screen, it wasn't from a spacecraft—you know, to see it for real with its rings was a sight that absolutely fired my imagination and it's stayed with me ever since. It seemed like it was the best view I've ever had of Saturn because it was the first. It was absolutely the sight of Saturn that just sparked that imagination, and set me on the journey that I had.

Q *What is your favorite planet, and why?*

A I would probably say Mars. The reason I say Mars is because it changes. When you look through a telescope, you can actually see things changing. Mars has polar caps, and as Mars goes through its seasons like we have on the Earth, you can actually see the polar caps growing and shrinking. You can see dust storms and, because Mars is like one big desert, sometimes these big dust storms whip up and obscure [hide] all the detail from the surface.

Q *Do you have any space heroes?*

A I think Galileo would have to be one. He was the first one to use a telescope on the night sky. I think he was probably one of the key people who made some big, big, big discoveries that changed our view of the universe. And, you know, he paid for it. He got arrested by the church and stuck in house arrest for a lot of years. But I think the things he did, and people like him, took us forwards in leaps and bounds in understanding the universe.

Q *What advice would you give to readers who want to be astronomers?*

A I would say, obviously, go with a responsible adult, don't go out on your own at nighttime. Use a pair of binoculars or a small telescope if you can get one. Just start looking, because there's an incredible world out there. If you can, either buy a planisphere or get one of these smart phone applications and start learning your way around the sky, and get out there and enjoy it. You know, there's loads of stuff that's in the sky that you can see that's really easy to find. It's a fantastic pastime and it means you can stay up late as well!

THE SPACE AGE

The first space flights took place in the mid-1900s, starting with trips into Earth's orbit. Countries began competing to explore the solar system.

Telescopes were sent into orbit around Earth, where they had a much better view of space. Robotic probes were sent to the planets. They used cameras, **radar**, and other instruments to collect as much information as possible.

Mariner 2 flew past Venus in 1962. It was the first spacecraft to visit another planet. It sent back information about the extreme surface temperatures.

GETTING THERE

When you fly to Mercury and Venus, you will have to overcome the challenges faced by the first robotic probes.

- Escaping Earth: A force called **gravity** attracts objects to each other. Bigger objects have stronger gravity. It is Earth's gravity that stops everything on it from floating off into space. Rockets are used to overcome this force and blast probes into space.

- Finding the planets: Venus zooms through space at 22 miles (35 kilometers) per second, and Mercury is even faster, at 31 miles (50 kilometers) per second. That is a solar system record! They do not stay in one place for long.

- Coping with heat: Mercury and Venus are much closer to the Sun, so you will need a super-tough spaceship and spacesuit to protect you from roasting heat and dangerous **radiation**.

AMAZING FACTS

Other planets are very hard to get to, even with robotic spacecraft. Humans were able to explore the Moon on foot before probes managed to photograph the surfaces of Mercury and Venus!

PHOTOGRAPHING THE PLANETS

Information collected by Venus and Mercury missions will help you on your own journey. You may even come across the remains of these probes.

MAPPING MERCURY

In 1974 and 1975, **NASA**'s *Mariner 10* probe took the first close-up photographs of Mercury's surface. In 2004, NASA launched the *Mercury Messenger* mission. Its tasks include looking for frozen water in deep craters on Mercury. It has sent back thousands of pictures of the surface.

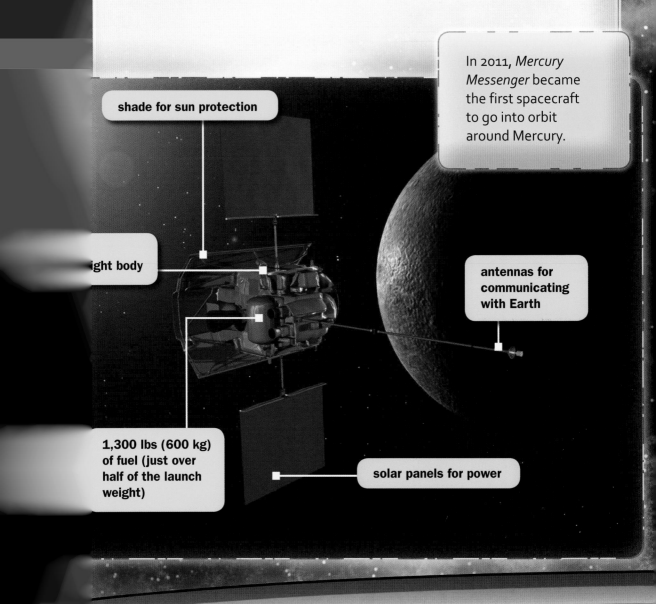

In 2011, *Mercury Messenger* became the first spacecraft to go into orbit around Mercury.

shade for sun protection

ight body

antennas for communicating with Earth

1,300 lbs (600 kg) of fuel (just over half of the launch weight)

solar panels for power

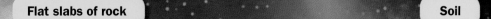

Flat slabs of rock

Soil

Venera 13 managed to take this photo of Venus's surface, before being destroyed by heat and **pressure**.

VISITING VENUS

Mariner 2 flew by Venus in 1962, and *Mariner 10* managed to snap a close-up on its way to Mercury. However, thick clouds made the surface invisible. No one knew what it looked like until 1975, when two *Venera* probes, sent by the **Soviet Union**, managed to land. They sent back a few black and white photographs. In 1981, two more *Venera* probes took color photographs and even studied the soil.

NASA's *Pioneer Venus* and *Magellan* probes used radar to "see through" Venus's clouds. Between 1990 and 1994, Magellan mapped 98 percent of the surface. The latest probe to visit Venus was the **European Space Agency's** *Venus Express*, which began orbiting the planet in 2006. Its mission was to study Venus's **atmosphere**. It also made the exciting discovery that volcanoes on Venus may still be active.

ALL ABOUT MERCURY AND VENUS

Scientists combined the amazing discoveries of Mercury and Venus probes with observations made from Earth. They figured out what each planet is made of, and what conditions are like on the surface. These are the facts you need to know before you go.

Mercury and Venus took tens of millions of years to form. Around 4.5 billion years ago, collections of rocky **particles** were smashed together in enormous collisions, forming huge lumps of **molten** rock and metal. Large parts of the planets have become solid as they cool.

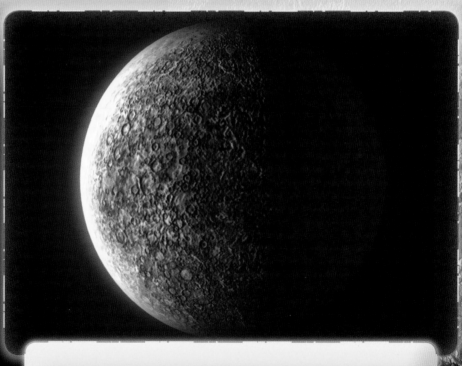

Mercury's rocky, cratered surface looks a bit like the Moon's.

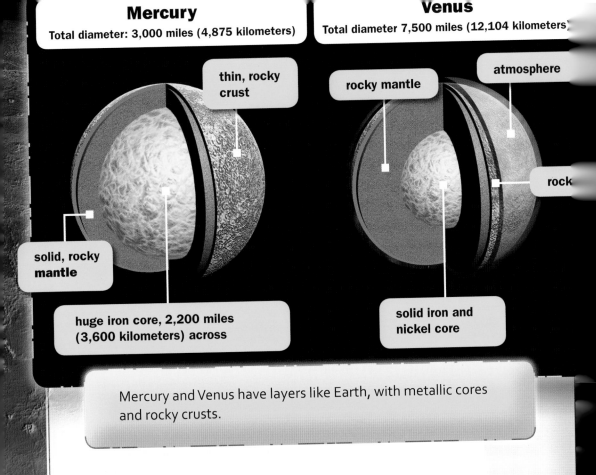

Mercury
Total diameter: 3,000 miles (4,875 kilometers)

thin, rocky crust

solid, rocky mantle

huge iron core, 2,200 miles (3,600 kilometers) across

Venus
Total diameter 7,500 miles (12,104 kilometers)

rocky mantle

atmosphere

rock

solid iron and nickel core

Mercury and Venus have layers like Earth, with metallic cores and rocky crusts.

METALLIC MERCURY

Mercury is packed with metals, especially iron. Its huge iron **core** is much bigger than expected for such a small planet. Scientists think that Mercury was once much bigger. One idea is that a giant **asteroid** blew off a large portion of the rocky **crust**. Another idea is that a sudden increase in the Sun's heat boiled off some of Mercury's surface!

VOLCANIC VENUS

Venus is a similar size to Earth, and it is also thought to be similar on the inside. Like Earth, it is still very hot at the center. The heat melts rocks deep inside Venus. In the past, the molten rock has exploded onto the surface as volcanoes.

RESET YOUR BODY CLOCK

Like Earth, Mercury and Venus are orbiting (traveling around) the Sun and spinning on their own **axes** at the same time. This means they have years, days, and nights. But the timings are very different from what you are used to.

Each trip that a planet takes around the Sun is known as a year. Because Mercury and Venus are closer to the Sun than Earth, it takes them less time to travel around it. Mercury has the shortest year—astronauts on Mercury would celebrate a New Year every 3 months!

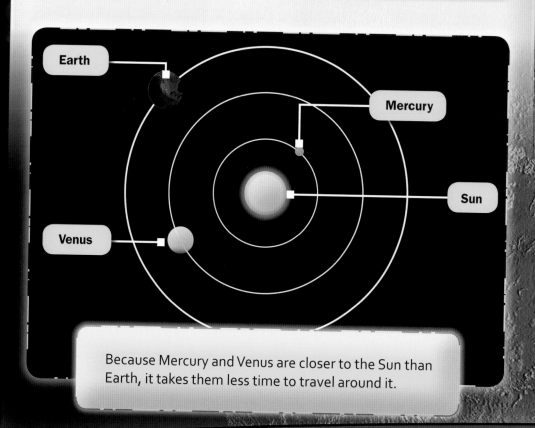

Because Mercury and Venus are closer to the Sun than Earth, it takes them less time to travel around it.

Mercury's egg-shaped orbit and slow rotation mean that in some places, the morning Sun rises briefly, sets, and rises again! The same thing happens at sunset.

IN A SPIN

Both planets spin as they travel, causing day and night. Mercury and Venus turn much more slowly than Earth.

Mercury can make two trips around the Sun in the time it takes to spin three times on its axis. Venus is the slowest-spinning planet in our solar system. It takes 243 Earth days to complete one spin. On Venus, a day (one spin) is longer than a year (one trip around the Sun)!

NUMBER CRUNCHING

Planet	Length of orbit/year	Time taken to spin once on axis (day)
Mercury	88 Earth days	59 Earth days
Venus	225 Earth days	243 Earth days
Earth	365 days	24 hours

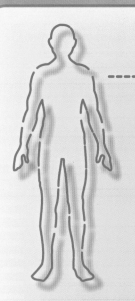

WHO'S GOING WITH YOU?

If you could put together a dream crew for your mission to Mercury and Venus, it might include some of these people.

CREW MEMBER:

ALBERT EINSTEIN (1879–1955)

Mercury has a "wobbly" orbit that changes position every time the planet circles the Sun. German scientist Einstein figured out why, and he correctly predicted how much Mercury's orbit would move. He could help you find Mercury.

POTENTIAL JOB:

Navigator

CREW MEMBER:

EUGENIOS ANTONIADI (1870–1944)

French astronomer Antoniadi became famous for his observations of planets using a telescope on Earth. In 1933, he was the first person to produce a detailed map of the surface of Mercury. His map gave us a lot of information about Mercury, although he did get some things wrong. Antoniadi named some of the surface features you will visit, and a ridge is named after him.

POTENTIAL JOB:

Tour guide on Mercury

CREW MEMBER:

CARL SAGAN (1934–1996)

U.S. astronomer Sagan worked on preparing early missions to Mercury and Venus. He made many important discoveries and helped to figure out why Venus is so hot. Most famously, he researched alien life and would know what signs to look out for!

POTENTIAL JOB:

Alien spotter/weather forecaster

CREW MEMBER:

NEIL ARMSTRONG (BORN 1930)

Mercury's cratered surface, low gravity, and thin atmosphere are similar to those on the Moon. Neil Armstrong was the first human to walk on the Moon. He could be a great help.

POTENTIAL JOB:

Health and safety officer

CREW MEMBER:

VOLCANOLOGIST

A volcanologist (person who studies volcanoes) would be able to help you deal with the harsh conditions on volcanic Venus, such as intense heat and clouds of stinky **sulfur dioxide**. A volcanologist would also be able to spot signs of active volcanoes!

POTENTIAL JOB:

Hazard spotting on Venus

TOUCHING DOWN

A planet's atmosphere is shaped by its size and distance from the Sun. What can you expect as you touch down on Mercury and Venus?

MERCURY'S THIN AIR

On Earth, we do not worry that the air we breathe is about to escape into space. But on Mercury, this is happening all the time! Mercury's small size means that it does not have enough gravity to trap gases for long. As the planet heats up in the sunlight, these gases zoom off into space.

DON'T FORGET

Bring a hard hat in case of meteoroid showers. Mercury's thin atmosphere does not "burn up" these pieces of falling dust and rock like Earth's atmosphere does. Objects as small as a grain of sand or as large as a boulder will hit the surface— or your head!

HARSH CONDITIONS

The lack of atmosphere makes Mercury's surface a harsh place to be. There is nothing to protect the planet from objects hurtling toward it in space. Craters from crashing **meteoroids** cover Mercury's dark and dusty surface. With nothing to shield the planet from the Sun, daytime temperatures rise to 800 degrees Fahrenheit (430 degrees Celsius). That is hotter than an oven. At night, there is nothing to stop this heat from escaping into space, so temperatures plunge to –290 degrees Fahrenheit (–180 degrees Celsius)—cold enough to freeze air!

Mercury's sights are named after Earth's most famous artists, authors, and musicians. You could soak up the sun in the Shakespeare Region, dine in Degas Crater, or "dust-board" down Beethoven Crater!

AMAZING FACTS

Be prepared for a shock at sunrise. From Mercury, the Sun looks up to three times bigger than it does from Earth!

VENUS

Landing on Venus means passing through fierce winds, clouds of sulfuric acid, and lightning. The surface is also not welcoming. Jagged rocks, enormous volcanoes, and scorched sand dunes are lit by a gloomy, orange glow.

AWFUL ATMOSPHERE

Venus has the opposite problem from Mercury. Its atmosphere is so thick and heavy that it presses down on the surface like a huge weight. The pressure at the surface is 90 times greater than it is on Earth. An astronaut would feel the same pressure as a diver deep under the ocean.

This artist's impression of Venus does not capture the nasty smell. Just like volcanoes on Earth, Venus's atmosphere smells like rotten eggs!

Venus is wrapped in a blanket of clouds 15 miles (25 kilometers) thick. The lower layers are made up of large drops of sulfuric acid, which can burn skin and **dissolve** metal. Acid rain falls from the clouds, but it turns into a gas again before it hits the surface of Venus.

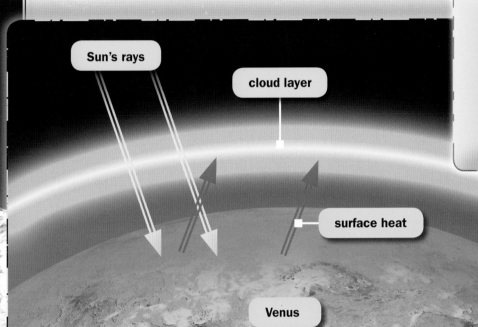

Sun's rays

cloud layer

surface heat

Venus

An extreme greenhouse effect keeps Venus hotter than Mercury, even though it is nearly twice as far from the Sun.

EXTREME HEAT

Thick clouds mean that Venus is always overcast. Just a fifth of the sunlight reaching Venus gets through to the surface. The clouds reflect most of the sunlight back into space. However, this does not help to keep the surface cool. The thick clouds trap the Sun's heat like glass traps heat in a greenhouse. This greenhouse effect keeps surface temperatures at around 867 degrees Fahrenheit (464 degrees Celsius), even at night. It makes Venus the hottest planet in the solar system.

Mercury's surface has been battered and cracked by natural processes. They created the famous features that you will see on your tour.

RIDGES AND CLIFFS

Mercury is crisscrossed with cliffs up to 2 miles (3 kilometers) high and hundreds of miles long. These steep ridges formed as the planet cooled and shrank, causing the crust to crack.

GHOST CRATERS

Mercury's surface is covered with craters, formed by asteroid and meteoroid strikes more than 3.5 billion years ago. Between the craters lie huge, flat plains of lava that oozed out of volcanic vents and cooled in pools. In some places, the solidified lava is a few miles thick. Some "ghost craters" have been filled in by flowing lava.

The Caloris Basin (shown here as a big, yellow area) is one of the largest craters in the solar system.

CALORIS BASIN

Around 3.8 billion years ago, an asteroid landed on Mercury, forming the huge Caloris Basin. The asteroid that created Caloris was at least 62 miles (100 kilometers) wide, and it left a crater 960 miles (1,550 kilometers) across.

DON'T FORGET

You may need an ice pick. Mercury's poles never receive sunlight, so temperatures there stay below −256 degrees Fahrenheit. Scientists believe there may be frozen water at the bottom of deep craters.

Caloris is one of the hottest places on Mercury—the name means "heat" in Latin. The basin floor is covered with small volcanoes, craters, and trenches. Visit the Brahms Crater to see the 2-mile- (3-kilometer-) high mountain peak in the center.

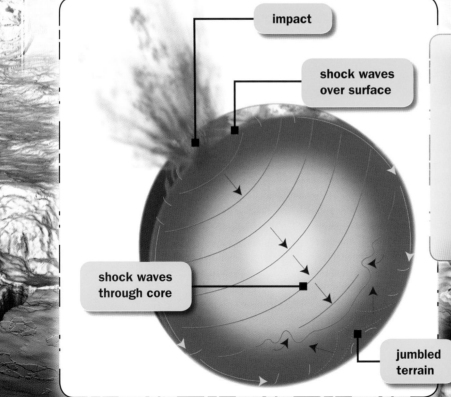

impact

shock waves over surface

shock waves through core

jumbled terrain

The impact that created Caloris sent shock waves through Mercury. On the other side of the planet, they caused huge earthquakes that shattered the surface. The area is known as the jumbled terrain.

WHAT TO SEE ON VENUS

Venus is covered with winding "rivers" and low-lying flood plains. They were not formed by water, but rather by red-hot molten rock! The planet is packed with volcanic features you will not find anywhere else in the solar system.

Volcanoes

More than 1,000 major volcanoes dot the surface of Venus. Most are clustered together in small hilly areas called regio. Eistla Regio is a must-see for its pancake domes. You will not find these weird, flat lava domes anywhere else in the solar system.

Maat Mons and Sapas Mons are volcanoes named after goddesses from different cultures. Maat Mons is the tallest volcano on Venus. At 5 miles (8 kilometers) above average surface level, it is twice as high as the largest active volcano on Earth!

Maat Mons

Sapas Mons

A computer created this 3D view of Venus's surface, using information collected by probes.

Highlands

Venus has two huge highland areas. Ishtar Terra is around the size of Australia, and Aphrodite Terra is even bigger—around the size of South America. For the best view of Ishtar Terra, climb Maxwell Montes on the eastern edge. This is the highest mountain on Venus.

DON'T FORGET

Watch where you walk! Scientists think that some of Venus's volcanoes may still be active. One wrong step and you could end up knee-deep in molten rock. People who study volcanoes on Earth often wear clothes made from heat-resistant asbestos, so maybe you should, too.

Venus's volcanic features include arachnoids. These unusual volcanoes have a dome surrounded by ridges and valleys that look like spider legs.

CRATER SPOTTING

Venus has far fewer craters than Mercury, and each one is more than 2 miles (1.5 kilometers) wide. The planet's thick atmosphere burns up small meteoroids before they can hit the surface. It also slows down any large meteoroids that do make it through, so the craters are wide but shallow.

Although Venus is a similar size to Earth, it has no **magnetic field**. This means a compass would be useless on the planet. An astronaut would have to find another way to navigate.

Lava has filled in many craters. The thousand or so that are left are unlike any others in the solar system. Some have unusual features created by molten lava flowing out of the crater, such as the mermaid's tail of the Addams Crater.

Don't miss seeing the mermaid's tail of the Addams Crater when you visit Venus!

OTHER FEATURES

You will also come across coronae. These large "blisters" of rock were formed by hot magma rising up under the surface without breaking through. The biggest is Artemis Corona, which is 1,600 miles (2,600 kilometers) across.

Maxwell Montes is the only site on Venus named after a man, in honor of James Clerk Maxwell (1831–1879). He was a Scottish scientist who made very important discoveries about light. Most sights on Venus are named after famous women from history or myths. These include Guinevere, Cleopatra, and Aphrodite.

Molten magma oozed from cracks and created long, winding channels. From a distance they look like rivers that are hundreds of miles long.

INTERVIEW WITH AN ASTRONAUT

Paolo Nespoli is an Italian astronaut with the European Space Agency (ESA). He enjoys scuba diving, flying airplanes, and photography. In 2007, Paolo went into space for 15 days, and in 2010 he spent another 6 months in space. In total, he has traveled more than 69 million miles (111 million kilometers).

Q *When you came back from the International Space Station, was it difficult to get used to not being weightless?*

A My first ride was ... 15 days. Coming back, I really felt the effects of gravity pretty heavily, and so I was wondering how I would feel when I came back after six months. Now I know it's pretty bad. I felt like I weighed 200 or 300 kilograms [about 450 to 650 pounds]. Just lifting my arm was something that I needed to do consciously and pay attention to it. I mean, I had a watch on and I felt the watch was weighing 3 kilograms [about 7 pounds] on my arm! Walking was very difficult, both because of the muscles [being weak], but also because of nausea, balance problems, all sorts of things like that.

Q *Would you prefer to be weightless all the time, if you could?*

A You learn after a while to float around like Spider-Man, from one wall to another wall, just pushing yourself … Of course, sometimes you misjudge the effort that it takes or the push that you push, so you go and slam into walls and other stuff. But this is part of the fun, I think. I find myself like a little kid, exploring, doing things in a different way. It was very nice to just float around, push here, push there, go here, go there, pick up something that weighs 300, 400, 500 kilograms [650 to 1,100 pounds], and just move it around like nothing.

On the other hand, it was really irritating that you can only handle two or three things, and then you start losing stuff. If you lose something, it doesn't go on the floor, it goes all around and it's difficult to find. It happened several times, I would be eating something—a little pouch with some food and a spoon—and suddenly the spoon is gone, or the food is gone! And two hours later you're passing by, and there is your spoon or your tuna floating right in the middle of the module!

Q *If you were talking to students, what would you tell them they need to really focus on learning if they want to be an astronaut?*

A I'd tell them, "You need to understand what you like, what you will be good at. Something that you can do all day and not be tired of, and be happy with what you are doing." It's almost like finding out what is your nicest hobby or most precious hobby and make it your work, so you are paid to do a hobby, and at the end of the day you are happy and not tired. You really need to find what makes you happy and make it your profession. And if this is being an astronaut, please go ahead.

COULD HUMANS LIVE ON MERCURY OR VENUS?

Although robot probes and powerful instruments on Earth have investigated other planets, no human has ever been to another planet. Could astronauts visit or even live on Mercury or Venus one day?

It would be very difficult. Earth has the perfect conditions for life. There is water to drink, **oxygen** to breathe, and enough sunlight to keep us warm without getting too hot. Venus has a similar size and structure to Earth, but conditions are very different. Without special protection, an astronaut would be crushed by the atmosphere, prevented from breathing by the poisonous air, boiled by high temperatures, or dissolved by acid rain!

DON'T FORGET

The air on Venus is mainly carbon dioxide, which is toxic to humans. Traces of sulfur dioxide also make it stinky. Mercury has a tiny bit of oxygen, but because the air pressure is very low, the oxygen is too widely spread out to breathe. So, on either planet you will need air tanks for breathing.

Mercury does not have a true atmosphere, so you will not have the same problems as on Venus. But that does not mean it is free of trouble. There is nothing to block the Sun's searing heat or radiation from space. It is not surprising that there are no signs of life on Mercury or Venus.

AMAZING FACTS

Even super-tough robot probes costing millions of dollars only survived for a few hours on Venus's surface. They were destroyed by the intense heat and pressure.

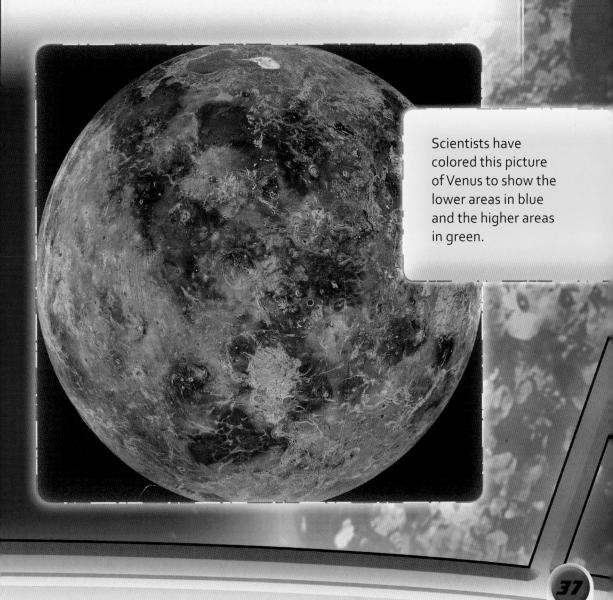

Scientists have colored this picture of Venus to show the lower areas in blue and the higher areas in green.

FUTURE EXPLORATION

Humans may not ever be able to live on Mercury and Venus, but that does not stop us from wanting to study them. Understanding the history and geology of these planets helps scientists to understand how Earth formed. It also helps them to hunt for planets near other stars in our galaxy.

ALL ABOARD FOR VENUS

Japan hopes that its *Akatsuki* probe will be the next spacecraft to orbit Venus. The probe arrived at the planet in 2010, but it did not slow down enough to enter orbit. Its next opportunity will come in 2016.

Once in orbit, *Akatsuki* will study Venus's thick clouds and look for active volcanoes.

BepiColombo will look out for asteroids close to the Sun.

NEXT STOP: MERCURY

The European Space Agency (ESA) will put a spacecraft into orbit around Mercury in 2019. *BepiColombo* will fly past Venus on its six-year journey to Mercury. Once it enters Mercury's orbit, it will study the planet for up to two years, answering questions about its structure, craters, magnetic field, and atmosphere. It will even look out for asteroids close to the Sun.

Each new mission to Mercury and Venus answers many questions, but it brings big surprises and new mysteries, too. What will you discover on your trip?

AMAZING FACTS

Some space trips are already being offered to the public. For several hundred thousand dollars, space tourists can zoom up to the edge of Earth's atmosphere for an astronaut's view of our planet.

MAP OF THE SOLAR SYSTEM

MERCURY

VENUS

EARTH

MARS

ASTEROID BELT

JUPITER

SATURN

URANUS

NEPTUNE

The sizes of the planets and their distances from the Sun are not to scale. To show all the planets' real distances from the Sun, this page would have to be over half a mile long!

TIMELINE

c. 3500–500 BCE Ancient Egyptians observe Mercury and Venus and call Mercury "Thoth," after their god of knowledge.

733 BCE Mayans record an observation of Venus as a morning "star."

727 BCE Mayans record an observation of Venus as an evening "star."

c. 450 BCE Ancient Greeks call Mercury two different names—Apollo (god of truth) and Hermes (messenger god of writing).

650 CE Mayans create a calendar based on the changing position of Venus in the night sky.

1610 Galileo Galilei is the first person to observe Venus through a telescope.

1933 Eugenios Antoniadi makes the first map of Mercury's surface, using a telescope.

1962 *Mariner 2* visits Venus and discovers how hot its surface is.

1965 Gordon Pettengill and Rolf Dyce use the Earth's *Arecibo* radio telescope to measure how fast Mercury spins.

1967 *Venera 4* enters Venus's atmosphere and discovers it is mainly made up of carbon dioxide.

1970 *Venera 7* lands on Venus and sends back data for 23 minutes before being destroyed by heat.

1974–1975 *Mariner 10* takes the first close-up pictures of Mercury's surface, but it can only photograph one side.

1981 *Venera 13* and *14* land on Venus and survive for 2 hours and 7 minutes. They send back color photographs and data about the soil.

1991 Scientists (based on Earth) spot signs of ice in cold craters at Mercury's north and south poles.

2006 *Venus Express* goes into orbit around Venus.

2008 *Mercury Messenger* flies past Mercury and begins to send back photographs of Mercury, including the side that was not seen by *Mariner 10*.

2011 *Mercury Messenger* goes into orbit around Mercury to study it more closely, with enough fuel to stay until 2013.

FACT FILE

	Mercury	Venus	Earth
Diameter	3,029 mi. (4,875 km)	7,521 mi. (12,104 km)	7,926 mi. (12,756 km)
Average distance from Sun	36 million mi. (58 million km), like flying from New York City to Sydney, Australia, 3,624 times	67 million mi. (108 million km), like flying from New York City to Sydney, Australia, 6,744 times	93 million mi. (150 million km), like flying from New York City to Sydney, Australia, 9,361 times
Surface temperature	−292 °F to 806 °F (−180 °C to 430 °C)	867 °F (464 °C)	59 °F (15 °C)
Air	52 percent oxygen 39 percent sodium vapor 8 percent helium 1 percent other gases (total amount of air is very small compared to Earth's air)	96.5 percent carbon dioxide 3.5 percent nitrogen and other gases (traces of water vapor, sulfur dioxide, argon)	78.1 percent nitrogen 20.9 percent oxygen 1 percent other gases (argon and traces of other gases)
Gravity	0.38 of Earth's gravity	0.9 of Earth's gravity	1
What would I weigh if I weigh 135 lbs (61 kg) on Earth?	Mercury's gravity is around one-third of Earth's gravity. This means that an astronaut's weight would also be around one third of his or her weight on Earth. For example, if you weigh 135 lbs (61 kg) on Earth, you will weigh just 50 lbs (23 kg) on Mercury.	Venus's gravity is only slightly less than Earth's gravity. This means that an astronaut would weigh slightly less than he or she does on Earth. For example, if you weigh 135 lbs (61 kg) on Earth, you will weigh 123 lbs (56 kg) on Venus.	135 lbs (61 kg)

GLOSSARY

asteroid small object in the solar system that is traveling on its own path around the Sun

astronomer person who studies space

atmosphere layer of gases surrounding a planet

axis (plural: **axes**) imaginary line that planets spin around

core central part of a planet

crater dish-shaped hole in the surface of a planet, made by a meteorite smashing into the surface

crust thin, rocky outer layer of a planet

data facts and statistics that have been collected

dissolve break down and become thoroughly mixed with a liquid

European Space Agency (ESA) European organization involved in space research and exploration

gravity force that pulls objects toward each other. Big objects, such as planets, have much stronger gravity than smaller objects, such as people.

instrument machine or tool for measuring something— for example, speed, temperature, or position

magnetic field region around a magnet where it has an effect on magnetic materials and other magnets

mantle area between the crust and core of a planet

meteoroid small piece of rock, metal, or ice orbiting the Sun

molten solid that has melted to become liquid

mythology stories and tales from ancient times, often involving heroic deeds and adventures

NASA short for "National Aeronautics and Space Administration," the U.S. space agency

observatory building with telescopes and other instruments for observing (looking at) stars and planets

orbit path of an object around a star or planet

oxygen gas needed by living things

particle very tiny object

pressure pushing force on an object from something touching it, such as the pushing force of the air on our bodies

probe robot spacecraft sent to visit planets, moons, and other objects in the solar system

radar system for "seeing" objects by sending out short bursts of radio waves, which bounce off the object

radiation particles and rays that come from some objects in space, such as stars. Some types of radiation are harmful to humans.

solar system the Sun, the planets, and other objects that are in orbit around it

Soviet Union name for an area of Asia and Eastern Europe that used to be one huge country, but is now made up of many separate countries

sulfur dioxide poisonous and smelly gas made out of sulfur and oxygen

telescope device that makes distant objects look bigger

universe everything that exists, including all of space and all the objects and energy in it

FIND OUT MORE

BOOKS

Bond, Peter. *DK Guide to Space* (DK Guides). New York: Dorling Kindersley, 2006.

Goldsmith, Mike. *Solar System* (Discover Science). New York: Macmillan, 2010.

Oxlade, Chris. *Mercury, Mars, and the Other Inner Planets* (Earth and Space). New York: Rosen Central, 2008.

Sparrow, Giles. *Earth and the Inner Planets* (Space Travel Guides). Mankato, Minn.: Smart Apple Media, 2012.

INTERNET SITES

FactHound offers a safe, fun way to find internet sites related to this book. All of the sites on FactHound have been researched by our staff.

Here's all you do:

Visit *www.facthound.com*

Type in this code: 9781410945716

PLACES TO VISIT

Hayden Planetarium
Central Park West and 79th Street, New York, N.Y. 10024
www.haydenplanetarium.org

Smithsonian National Air and Space Museum
Independence Ave. at 7th St. SW, Washington, D.C. 20560
www.nasm.si.edu

SIGHTS TO SEE

You can spot Mercury and Venus in the sky at dawn and dusk. Venus is very bright and easy to spot. Mercury is harder to see, because it is fainter and visible for just a few days every month. If you look for the planets yourself, make sure that the Sun is not in the sky at the same time. Looking at the Sun can damage your eyes.

FURTHER RESEARCH

Type these names into a search engine to get a sneak preview of more famous sites on Mercury and Venus:

Mercury	Venus
Caloris Basin	Maxwell Montes
Discovery Rupes	Eistla Regio pancake domes
Brahms Crater	Sachs Patera
Degas Crater	Gula Mons
Firdousi Crater	Sapas Mons
Beagle Rupes	Dali Chasma
Verdi Crater	Cleopatra Crater
Bek Crater	Addams Crater

INDEX